Developing quicker via

doing much less

I0504661

BY

HARVEY VICTOR

TABLE OF CONTENT

DESCRIPTION

It may seem a contradiction, but the evidence is overwhelming that companies that focus on doing more and more outsourcing grow exponentially faster than those who prefer to do things in -house. It is an approach that can help accelerate the growth of your company. The rapid rise of organizations such as Google, Airbnb, Uber and Tesla have encouraged people to reconsider what is necessary to be a successful organization, inspiring books such as the exponential organization of Salim Ismail. But they are not only these new organizations that have discovered that more and more outsourcing is the recipe for success. The Hollywood film industry is a good case of study of a consolidated industry that has used this model to transform itself to meet the needs of a world that changes for over half a century. So why doesn't everyone do it? There is a real danger for companies that don't adopt this business model because, like the cab industry versus Uber, they fall victim to those that do. With such a compelling case for taking this approach, it's reasonable to ask why more companies aren't jumping on board.

Chapter 1.The main barrier to adoption is mindset

Individually and collectively, people in organizations are reluctant to proactively seek disruptive change. By thinking of the world as it is instead of as it could be, they limit themselves to creating a faster caterpillar rather than turning into a butterfly. Some organizations only consider disruptive changes when they are forced upon them. This is often because adapting to disruptive change is seen as high risk and pain with little reward. The irony is that if they had proactively chosen to do this within their timeframe, rather than as a last resort, it would be far less painful, risky, and have a far greater chance of success.

Changing the organizational mindset is not easy. Typically, this starts with the realization that the organization already outsources some aspect of its business – that's why it has suppliers. It also helps when people within the organization truly understand the purpose of the business. It's been a hot topic on Ted Talks and in organizations in general for the past five years, but unfortunately most businesses still have a long way to go. Too often, companies rearrange the "why", "how", and "what" in their current worldview without opening themselves to the possibility of a different future.

A clear example is a business owner who insists on doing everything himself. Their business would be limited to a skill set and the amount of work they can do personally. Pride, fear, lack of confidence, inexperience, or just personal preference could lead someone to this approach. Whatever their reasoning, the fact remains that if they don't get help, the profits and potential of their business will be limited.

Chapter 2.Redefining the boundaries

The outsourcing mentality forces you to stop defining the functions of the organization in terms of who performs them and how. Focus on what needs to be delivered to the customer first. Then consider everything that needs to be done for this to happen. Airbnb recognized that people needed homes. They also felt that they didn't need to provide hosting to deliver real value to customers. In doing so, Airbnb has redefined the boundaries of the hospitality industry – removing a major constraint and overhead from its business.

Every function of a business can be outsourced. Businesses are available to take customer calls, do bookkeeping, bookkeeping, transportation, sales, marketing, IT, product design, manufacture of goods, and even own the building where the business operates. or the equipment used. The discussion should not be about whether something can be outsourced, but how and by whom the best result for the client can be achieved - taking into account all internal and external possibilities. This is a discussion that will help you refine your understanding of your organization's unique value proposition and purpose.

Begin

Different books have different words and phrases to describe how to replicate the success of the latest world success stories. The underlying principle is simple:If you're not adding value internally, find a way to outsource it.Most business functions consist of three elements: people; systems; and process. View every function of your company. Evaluate whether each function should be done in-house or if it is better to do it outside. Transportation is a great example to start with: delivering products to customers is a critical function, but does your business add customer value by doing this internally?

Once you've compiled a list of functions that need to be performed internally, ask the same question of the people, systems, and processes within each function. There are many examples of companies using external systems. For example, word processor or accounting package. Outsourcing people and processes can be more difficult for companies. Franchising offers examples of both: the franchisor outsources people; and the affiliate outsources the processes.

The franchise divide brings a different lens through which you can look at your outsourcing strategy: Do you want to outsource business as usual or do you want to switch companies? Many organizations outsource elements of business change, as this often requires a temporary influx of capacity. IT and engineering projects are a typical example of this. There are also irregular BAU functions that are regularly outsourced, such as accounting and legal requirements. Similarly, most organizations use external marketing resources to help with large projects or campaigns. While these examples show that most companies have embraced outsourcing to some extent, it is rare for companies to adopt it as a competitive advantage.be brave

To truly grow faster by doing less, an organization must understand the ecosystem it operates in and determine how to maximize the value it delivers with minimal internal resources. Airbnb sells more beds per night than the biggest hotel chains, but it doesn't own a single hotel. Uber sells more rides per day than the largest taxi fleet, but employs no drivers. What does your company do for your customers? How can you deliver more value with fewer internal resources? In a highly connected world, there are more and more functions that you can outsource to specialized organizations at a lower cost than hiring staff, with the benefit of greater skills and expertise. Some organizations are reluctant to adopt this approach because they experience a loss of control, but the opposite is true: employees are required by law to try; while outsourced vendors are required by law to do so.

Keep it all together

An essential part of ensuring your business can grow quickly is understanding how to easily control all the moving parts, both internal and external. Uber manages the payment process, matches people to rides, and allows matched riders to track and rate their experience. With this, they made sure to control the process. When you look at your own business, what keeps you in control?

We live in a rapidly changing world. For a business to thrive in this new world, it must leverage the capabilities of other businesses. Don't ask where you need help, ask who does it best, if not, outsource it. This allows you to focus more on what you do best. This way, you create the best outcome for your customers and they will love you. Surround yourself with stars and you will shine.

Chapter 3.Overcoming obstacles to growth

Most companies want to grow, but few reach their full potential. What distinguishes those who reach their potential from those who don't is that the successful ones manage to overcome the three main obstacles to growth. Barriers are not hidden and cannot be avoided, they must be addressed. This article looks at the obstacles to growth and provides tips for overcoming them. 1. Delivering on standards and delivering on promises at higher volumes

We all know that talent only takes you so far. As they say, hard work beats talent until talent works hard. But even hardworking talent has its limits. After that point, the standards and promises you made to your customers simply cannot be delivered. This is a common barrier to growth, and to truly unlock the potential of your business, you need to move from relying on people to relying on processes. To illustrate this point, imagine how you would bake a single cake, then imagine how a pastry chef would bake a thousand cakes a day. The first method is very person-dependent, the second method is very process-dependent. Although you're probably not in the cake industry, you still need to make significant adjustments to your systems, processes, policies, and organizational structure to grow your business.

One of the first warning signs that a company is overcoming internal capacity is increased pressure on employees. The famous "Peter-Principal" states that a person is promoted to a position above his optimum capacity. In a fast growing business, although the effect is always the same, this principle works in reverse as the role trumps the person. A key tip here is to keep job titles humble, it makes it much easier to place new talent in leadership positions without having to "demote" loyal employees. Ideally, think ahead and design (or revise) your organizational structure for a larger version of the business, then assign employees the roles they will have in the larger business.

A key tip for managing your systems and processes is to enforce the use of current systems and processes, while treating them as temporary. This helps to make a clear distinction between work in the business (deploying systems and processes) and work on the business (changing systems and processes). Ideally, each change is done cleanly so that business moves quickly and smoothly from the old normal to a new normal. The best way to do this is to work at the pace of business.

2. Changes to Terms and Conditions and Margins

One of the dangers of a growing business is that it can be so focused on monitoring day-to-day operations that what happens outside the business doesn't get as much attention as it should. While the first hurdle was aimed at overcoming internal capacity limitations, overcoming this second hurdle requires greater attention to the outside world. Every business exists in an economic ecosystem. It is therefore important to understand the ecosystem or ecosystems that your company is a part of. It's also important to monitor your ecosystem on a regular basis, especially for important changes from other participants within the ecosystem, such as customer preferences and behavior, competitor positioning and offerings, as well as pricing and trustworthiness. of suppliers. Knowing the major turning points and bottlenecks in your ecosystem can help you make the right strategic decisions. An example of this is the formation of the Rockefeller empire. Realizing that the major bottleneck in the oil industry was the tankers, Rockefeller focused on taking over the railroads in order to control the oil industry. Most of its competitors were internally focused on oil exploration, but by the time they realized what was happening, it was too late for many of them. The dissolution of the Rockefeller empire by the US government may have restored competition to the industry, but not before most of his original competitors had perished and he had established his company as a leader in industry.

Here are some key questions for you:

Do you monitor the outside world? Do your management reports contain external data? Do you intend to examine possible scenarios? Do you monitor what your customers want? Is what you sell always what your customers want? Does what you sell align with your strategic direction? 3. Sales and marketing methods that don't scale

This is a very similar hurdle to the first, in that too often sales and marketing depend on people rather than systems and processes. Most of the top five reasons for poor sales are process-related. There is also a surprising reluctance from companies to invest in sales and marketing systems. There's no doubt that the sales team's general resistance to adopting systems and processes is a factor, but the lack of systems leaves companies too reliant on individual salespeople.

From the customer's perspective, sales and marketing are a continuum, but internally it requires delineation and cooperation. Good advice in this area is a clear separation between marketing and sales. The simplest is that marketing is one-to-many and sales is one-to-one. Done right, marketing is much more profitable than sales and much easier to scale. So another key tip here is to look for ways to transfer responsibilities and activities from the sales team to the marketing team. Typically, with the right system, only the top 20% of customers need to be managed, the rest can be managed by marketing. Each company can overcome these three significant obstacles of growth if it is able to manage in a proactive manner. Too often, the daily requirements of a business are accidentally prioritized in its long -term future.

Chapter 4.Top 5 Reasons for Bad Sales

Is your business reaching its sales potential? Most companies don't know. Of course, if you avoid the top five reasons for poor sales, you're more likely to do better than most. 1. Leaky Sales Pipeline

How visible is your sales pipeline? Do you know what's in the pipeline and where and why potential sales are leaking out as missed opportunities? Simply put, if you can't see and understand the problem, you can't fix it. If you can see and understand your sales pipeline and where it's leaking, you need to proactively monitor and fix leaks.

Great if you proactively monitor your sales pipeline and fix leaks

If not, you are not alone and have the potential to improve your sales

2. Sales pipeline blocked

A stalled sales pipeline differs from a leaky pipeline in that your prospects know and like you, but still don't buy. Do you know why? Is it because they are not convinced/interested (credibility, value, relevance)? Is it because it's too difficult to activate (complex buying process)? Or too hard to implement (clunky, hard to understand)? Each of these blocks can be solved, but you need to understand them first. Great if you know how to help customers buy from you. If not, you are not alone and have the potential to improve your sales

3. Broken promises

American sales guru Jack Daly says "Sales is the transfer of trust." It is the job of sales and marketing to deliver on promises and the role of the operational/delivery teams is to deliver. Failure to deliver on promises you make will inevitably lead to bad customer relationships, impacting repeat sales and your reputation in the marketplace. Does your sales and marketing team understand perfectly what you can promise and send your promises to operating / delivery teams? Do you have quality controls to make sure your promises are held to your customers?

Bravo if you are sure that your organization holds the promises you make for your customers. Otherwise - you are not alone and have the potential to improve your sales

4. Hidden Treasure

"Build it and you come" is fiction, it makes no sense to be a hidden treasure - you could be the best, but if your potential customers do not know you, you cannot buy them at home. What fuels your sales pipeline is making sure your prospects know you. Where once it was about localization, this will increasingly require a multi-tactical and multimedia approach. Do you know who your potential customers are and make sure they know you?

Great if you are sure that your potential customers know you and think highly of you. If not, you are not alone and have the potential to improve your sales

5. Badly constructed numbers

How much science is there in setting your prices and sales budget? Many companies set their sales budgets and prices with more hope than science, without monitoring the positions of their competitors. The sales team then inherits the budget and prices. They will then individually assess the likelihood of being able to complete the objectives that trigger the bonuses. If the target is set too low, they will only do what is necessary to trigger the bonuses (perhaps holding back some to ensure they can trigger the next bonus). If the goal is set too high, which is the most common mistake, the sales team gives up on ambitious goals and goes straight for job security, at your organization or elsewhere.

Good if you have well thought out and reasoned price points and sales targets. If not, you are not alone and have the potential to improve your sales

Nearly every business has the potential to improve their sales with a few sales and/or marketing changes. If you've identified an opportunity to improve more than one of the top five reasons for poor sales described above, you may find it easier to fix them one by one. Prioritize what you think will cost you the most revenue and fix it first. Once you've ticked them all, don't get depressed, think about the opportunity to grow! Likewise, if you don't know where to start, make sure you don't break your promises. Then proceed to monitor and repair the leaky sales funnel and then unclog it. Some would say you should raise awareness first, but there's little point in guiding prospects through a leaky or blocked sales pipeline—it'll only damage your reputationwith them and make it harder to sell to them later on.

Chapter 5.Key sales statistics

Digital marketing has introduced many new metrics and has made marketing much more focused on metrics. Meanwhile, sales live or die by hitting the revenue target. But if you really want to improve your sales and marketing results, there is one key point: the efficiency of the sales cycle. Sales cycle efficiency (SCE) is a multiple of the conversion rate at each stage of the sales cycle. The reason this metric is so useful is that it brings into focus the weakest links in your sales cycle. This is because zero multiplied by infinity is still zero.In practice, the number is much lower, usually 1 to 10. Since 10 is 10 times better than 1, any improvement to your SCE will have a significant impact on your bottom line.Calculate your current SCETo calculate your current SCE, you need to collect the following measurements over a period of time (for example, a month):

new questions / # confirmed contacts

quotes / # questions

sales / # quotes

deliveries / # sales

payments / # deliveries

requests from existing customers / # customers In some cases these figures can be as high as 100%, for example if all sales have been delivered and all deliveries have been paid for. However, this is a rare occurrence: even if things are prepaid, it is possible to issue refunds or cancel orders. Likewise, with an online store, you might think you're not doing quotes — but an abandoned checkout is the equivalent of a quote.Once you have these numbers, simply multiply them and multiply them by 100,000 to calculate your SCE score.Improve your ECS

The fastest way to improve your SCE is to focus on the weakest links – the sales stages with the lowest conversion rates. Look for the underlying factors that make the difference between moving to the next step or not. Then, put actions in place to address these factors. We have identified five key factors to evaluate:

Order value

Time spent in the sales stage

Customer relationship

Number of customer interactions

Customer service charges

Each of these has been shown to have an impact on the customer's willingness to move forward in the sales cycle. For example, new customers often have a mental limit on how much they are willing to spend (risk) on their first order. A customer who has been waiting for a quote for a long time may also choose to go to a competitor who responds more quickly.

The slightly different metric is cost of service. This factor is included to analyze whether costs have a material impact on success. If not, it indicates an opportunity to reduce acquisition costs.

Keeping it in perspective

Success in sales and marketing is essential to any business and the factors that determine that success are many and varied. Every company would like to have the demand for their product that Apple had before the first iPhone, when thousands of people lined up to become customers. But that moment in history is memorable because it's rare.

Aligning your sales and marketing conversations with how you can improve your SCE will drive improved performance. Areas of systemic failure such as lead capture, question answering, quote follow-up, new customer acquisition, and existing customer care are particularly common areas of improvement that can significantly improve SCE.

It's easy to get distracted by the vast amount of data and statistics now available to us. In a world overrun with data, it's important to focus on the metrics that matter. In sales and marketing, there are three: revenue, acquisition cost, and sales cycle efficiency. In sports terms, revenue is the ranking, but sales cycle efficiency is how you put that score on the scoreboard. our clients

Privacy Policy

Once a lead reaches a certain threshold based on key events, it can be promoted in the sales process from a marketing-qualified lead to a sales-qualified lead and approached by sales teams.

4. Run A/B tests to optimize underperforming segments. Ok, now that you've built your list of leads, segmented and qualified based on their

demographic/signature information and activity, it's time for content marketing to begin!

Start by creating content that appeals to each segment you created in Step 2, and distribute this content across social media channels, Google Ads, and wherever your target audience encounters them.

If the content is underperforming for a particular segment, try strategically changing key elements (like images, posts, or CTAs) to see if you can influence higher click-through rates for that content. [Need new ideas? Check out our guide to improving B2B display ad performance!]

5. Leverage customer-facing content like case studies and testimonials. While there are many different lead generation strategies for content marketing, customer reviews and testimonials are among the most powerful lead generation tools at your disposal.

Simply put, 88% of consumers trust reviews as much as personal recommendations, and trust these reviews 12 times more than product descriptions and sales copy. In fact, 95% of people say reviews (positive or negative) influence their buying decisions, and 70% of consumers say they trust a recommendation from someone they don't even know.

Case studies and testimonials are so effective because they essentially act as your own curated reviews. They allow your potential prospects to see how your product or service has helped another business achieve their goals, and they also provide hard data to validate the value of your product or service.

When designing your case studies, be sure to include meaningful statistics that are relevant to your customers and place them prominently so they're easy to find. Also, don't be afraid to write a testimonial copy and submit it to your client for approval. This usually ensures that you get a quality testimonial, and your client will appreciate not having to write anything from scratch.

Again, don't forget to share these case studies and testimonials on social media platforms, Google ads, and elsewhere to generate leads. If possible, redirect them to a landing page with a lead form.

Benefits of using intent data

6. Use intent data to improve your lead-scoring model and learn more about your target audience. We have previously touched the intent data briefly, but they can be used in various ways to make the Lead generation process more effective.

[What are the intent data? Find out here!]

Without intent data, your SDRs will fix a list of equally weighted leads without a good guide from whom you should first call or what you should say.

The intention data solve both problems showing the importance of interest, interesting activities and topics and topics of each account. By integrating the integration data into the Lead generation process, your SDRs have a list of priorities with sales leads, they will know in what topics every lead is interested and can adapt their awareness as a result. [See the complete beginner's guide to intent data here for the full scoop!]

7. Customize your brand communications based on your platform. Each of the major social media platforms has its own look and feel, so it's important to adopt some social media marketing principles when crafting your ads and creating the platform on which your ad will appear.

Create an ad on Instagram? Lead with visual material. Post on LinkedIn? Use a carousel ad!

Keeping the platform feel in mind when creating content will help you get more leads because your ads can leverage each platform's strengths and align with what your potential leads expect to see.

8. Evaluate, rinse and repeat. Lead generation is not a one-time thing; it is a continuous process.

Your list of leads will change constantly, with accounts going in and out of business. That's a good thing – it means more opportunities to generate more leads for your sales and marketing teams and ultimately convert more leads into customers. For this reason, it is important to continue to monitor your lists and results and keep your marketing of fresh content.

You must always generate new content, including case studies and testimonies, as you continue to convert customers via the funnel. This additional content will continue to improve your overall content.

Is the generation of leads the right strategy for you? If you want to meet the demand already in the funnel, the generation of leads is certainly an excellent strategy for your business. By following the eight steps above, you can start efficiently converting your high-quality leads into customers and quickly see business value across your sales process.

You may be amazed at the wide variety of types of business growth strategies and innovative ways to grow your business.

From financial growth models to marketing growth models, you have plenty of opportunities to dramatically increase sales or even launch the next game-changing expansion.

On this page:

Chapter 6.17 business growth strategy ideas (with concrete example)

First, let's explain what a business growth strategy is.It is simply a long-term plan to develop and sustain your business growth and gain greater market share.It is clear that the end goal is to generate more sales and revenue. However, a successful growth strategy is much more than that.It enables you to gain a sustainable competitive advantage, helps you communicate the value of your products, gets your teams working towards goals, enables you to reach new markets and reduce risk.For a growth strategy to be successful, you need to leverage many areas of your business, such as marketing, finance, operations, and research and development.A growth strategy usually begins with brainstorming ideas and capitalizing on new opportunities.Here we've gathered a list of powerful, cutting-edge, and innovative business growth strategy ideas to inspire you:

1. innovation strategy

Why innovate?

One of the oldest keys to any successful business is the ability to come up with new or unique ideas to keep offerings fresh.They recreate existing products and turn them into trendy new products that retain customers and attract new prospects.When you turn these ideas into reality, you create innovations.Nowadays, every company claims to be super innovative and modern. Then you have a much bigger job to try and deliver a product or service that customers can expect new values from.Now doing innovation is one of the most sustainable growth path as people constantly want more new products with super features.Innovations are simply crucial to success!

A successful innovation strategy can increase workplace productivity, make people remember your brand, help you unlock value, create a path for creative thinking in your organization, and make you stand out from the crowd.

Example:

One of the best examples of world-renowned companies that never stop innovating are: Google, Amazon, Microsoft, Apple, Samsung, Tesla, Nike, P&G, Hewlett Packard, Alibaba just to name a few.Take Samsung, the world leader in chip technology, battery and design. Your innovations seem endless.

They have the first foldable OLED display, the first ultra-thin dual-sided LCD, and more. Samsung always demonstrates exceptional design and engineering in cutting-edge technology.How to be innovative? Some possibilities and ideas:Be prepared to invest money in research and development activities

Observe customers and ask for ideas Use difficulties and complaints as a starting point for innovation Watch the competition Ask your employees for ideasHire innovative people

Don't just innovate, differentiate yourself

Renew not only your products, but also your workplace

2. Legendary customer service and customer service This is how legendary customer service works Why?

Today more than ever, customers demand good service. Because of this, creating a customer care plan is one of the strongest examples of competitive advantage today.The ability to create exceptional and memorable customer service is available to almost any business if they genuinely care about their customers' experience.Unhappy customers will not let your business grow. Quite the opposite.Don't just sell to customers. You also provide them with excellent customer service and after-sales support. Think of your organization as a constant way to keep your customers happy.Guide them on an enjoyable and memorable customer journey.

Example:

For example, online shoe retailer Zappos offers one of the best service experiences. They respond to customer emails at an incredibly fast speed. They don't discuss returns.And they even shop from other stores for customers if they want something specific that isn't in Zappos' stock.How to provide excellent customer service? Some possibilities and ideas:

Give your customers a platform to express themselves (e.g. live chat on your website)Conduct marketing intelligence to understand your customers' preferences, experiences and habitsIntegrate a rewards system into your customer service strategyAlways ask for feedback

Show respect and listen carefully. Train your employees on it. Respond as soon as possible Always think your customer is for life

3. Uniqueness

To succeed in our business environment where nearly all markets are crowded, the trick isn't to be first - it has to be both unique and hard to duplicate.If you can't be unique, there's no reason for customers to buy from you over your competitors. To be unique, you have to find a way to be different and even better than everyone else. Your business doesn't have to be a cliché.A unique product offers features and benefits with unique value for customers.

Example:

For example, Tesla Motors is unique because it not only sells cars, but also offers new technologies. If you choose Tesla Motors, you must choose powerful new technology. Tesla creates and dominates the market for long-range luxury electric automobiles. However, this market is different from the cheaper electric vehicle market as well as the luxury gasoline vehicle market. It is a unique proposition.

The way your business operates defines how unique it is.

How to make your business unique:

You can create uniqueness in many aspects of your business:In the quality of your work In prices In the course of delivery In personal connection with your customers In superlative support, etc.

4. Simplicity For what?

For many leading companies, offering simple products is one of the most important ways to grow and outperform their competitors.

Google's search engine, Apple's white headphones, and WhatsApp messaging are just a few of the products that deliver world-renowned great simplicity.

Less is more today. Simple products or processes save people time, effort and nerves.In our noisy, fast-paced lives, people are desperate for super-simple, automated products that require very little attention.

Making simple products that make life easier for customers is one of the modern growth strategies that works effectively.

Example:

Aldi, the world-renowned grocer based in Germany, provides a hassle-free shopping experience without confusing customers with complex promotions – it's at the heart of Aldi's simplicity.

The company strives to understand the variations in size desired by its audience and only offers the range that its customers actually need.

Being able to save customers time and money when shopping is a key competitive advantage, as it allows customers to spend more time and money with friends and family. How to ensure simplicity? Ways and Ideas:

- ★ Invest in state-of-the-art technology
- ★ Use Automation
- ★ Realize a simple product design

* ★ Create a user-friendly interface
* ★ Focus on function rather than features
* ★ Focus on a single consumer need

5. Talent acquisition and management.There's one thing that all the best companies in every industry have: talent.The best companies have the best employees. As a result, these companies can provide you with the best products and services.

Whatever industry you work in, you should view people as your most valuable asset.Talented passionate people who are committed to their careers are the candidates you want to hire. Example:

SAS's Employer of Choice and Talent Management strategy is breathtaking with outstanding results. They have been to 60 Minutes more times than any other company for excellent employee practices.They are known for their wide range and variety of benefits that ensure industry-leading revenue.

* ★ Talent management tips and ways
* ★ Find, hire and train talent
* ★ Create an attractive culture for talent to retain them
* ★ Use talent management and forecasting systems
* ★ Create a reward system for high performing employees
* ★ Develop job description and key roles
* ★ Offer opportunities for staff
* ★ Self-motivation help
* ★ Provide a workplace where employees are free to express their ideas

6. Company Information,This is one of the most powerful, innovative and sustainable business growth strategies today.In recent years, data analytics and Business Intelligence (BI) have become an important asset for any company that wants to reach the next level.

BI is a technology-driven process that allows you to analyze data and transform it into actionable information that you can use for successful data-driven decision making.

Today, BI is critical to business success because it helps you understand customer behavior, uncover buying patterns and sales trends, optimize processes, and even predict sales and financial results.

Example:

There are many examples of BI and data mining. Chipotle Mexican Grill (the famous American restaurant chain with more than 2400 establishments worldwide) has switched to BI software which allows it to have a centralized view of all restaurant operations.Previously, their disparate data sources didn't allow teams to have a unified view of restaurants. With the new BI solution, they can track operational efficiency at the national level.

As a result, report delivery speeds have tripled and saved thousands of hours. Additionally, Chipotle can now take understanding to the next level. How to set up and use BI? Ways and Ideas:

★ Hire a Chief Data Officer (CDO) and specialists with the right data scientist skills and qualifications
★ Choose the right software tools for your business, e.g. B. Customer intelligence tools, BI reporting tools, etc. Defining ways to collect data
★ Implement data management best practices in your organization
★ Use the services of leading data mining companies
★ Clean up your existing data
★ Develop a "data dictionary"

7. Content Marketing. This is one of the most exciting, powerful and sustainable business growth strategies you can think of today.Every second, an unimaginable number of consumers search online for products,

services and solutions. And if you could position your business in front of them, you would have a huge competitive advantage.

How do you market your business to online customers? With a strong content marketing strategy!

Content marketing allows you to attract, engage and delight customers by providing valuable content. It has many types and forms such as blogs, social media posts, podcasts, videos, infographics, white papers, case studies, eBooks, guides, webinars, email marketing, etc.Content marketing can boost your sales by giving your customers what they need while actively searching for it online.

So many businesses take their marketing campaigns to the next level through high quality blog posts, powerful social media posts, engaging videos, exciting webinars, etc.

Example:

For example, Charmin (the toilet paper brand) has a unique and one of the best example of content marketing. Charmin created an app called Sit or Squat for their customers. They have built a solid social media campaign around this app to populate it. The app allows users to check and rate the cleanliness of any public restroom. So people can check the toilets closest to them to see if they are clean or not.

It allows consumers to participate in the content experience themselves.The content is creative and funny. It shows you how to create great content that gets to the heart of your customers' challenges and provides a simple and effective solution. Tips for successful content marketing

Creating a sustainable content marketing strategy includes activities such as:

- ★ Define the best content channels for your business
- ★ Define the best content types and formats
- ★ Hire content marketing experts
- ★ Create a content calendar
- ★ Create an excellent blog with valuable and useful content
- ★ Create case studies
- ★ Use content marketing software, etc.

8. Craft as a strategy, Believe it or not, craftsmanship is still playing a role in our digital world and growing. Craftsmanship is more in demand than ever.

Now it seems like everything we buy is mass produced. People crave crafts or something truly unique. Faster is not always better. Additionally, today's generation craves authenticity - whether that's in search of organic foods, artisan products, or a celebration of art.

If you choose a craft strategy, you must dedicate your business to a tradition of excellence – delivering creative, unique, and even stunning products.

Example:

Harley-Davidson (motorcycles) is one of the most popular examples of how a handcrafted strategy works to create exceptional and lasting competitive advantage.

Today, almost everyone recognizes the classic chopper styling of a Harley.

Ways to improve your crafting strategy:

Create something that will be perceived as special, unique, unusual or extraordinary

- ★ Achieving perfection through mastery of detail
- ★ Offer products that evoke a sense of intimacy and harmony

- ★ Make quality your top priority
- ★ Give your products a real, unconventional and original look
- ★ Present the know-how of your products online

9. The strategy of speed and time. As technology accelerates nearly every aspect of our lives, it seems we consumers are addicted to instant gratification.We want instant connection, instant satisfaction, and we demand that it all be delivered now.Instant gratification culture is here to stay and you can use it to build a sustainable business growth strategy.

In business, speed can be of different types such as speed to market, fast delivery or fast service. You just have to do something faster than the competition. Examples:

Amazon Prime, UberEATS, and Jimmy John's are just a few examples of companies gaining a powerful competitive edge by making speed their number one priority.How to offer speed? Ways and ideas:

- ★ A speed strategy may require activities such as:
- ★ Shorten your production and your time-to-market
- ★ Implement shorter life cycles
- ★ Use faster and cheaper production technologies
- ★ Take advantage of new delivery channels, etc.

10. Reliability. It's human nature to always seek reliability. What we like the most is the reliability.

Every day we demand reliable cars that save on repairs, reliable cell phone service to stay connected, reliable suppliers that deliver on time, reliable restaurants with quality food, and more.Serving customers reliably is one of the increasingly modern competitive advantages and the key to business growth strategies.We all know the consequences of dealing with unreliable companies. They cost us time, money, stress and frustration.

Example:

Toyota and Lexus, for example, are so popular for their reliability that they move into sort of a different realm than the competition.

Toyota keeps its product updates simple, without trying complicated things at the same time with new models. More complexity sometimes means less reliability.

How do you make your company reliable? Ways and Ideas:

- ★ Build reliable teams and inspire them
- ★ Create reliable services and products
- ★ Ensure prompt response to business emails or customer calls
- ★ Invest in the manufacture of quality products
- ★ Commit to the highest level of security

11. Creativity. With the advent of new technologies, customers are always on the lookout for improved products that will make their lives happier, easier, more interesting or more adventurous. And delivering those products takes creativity.A creative corporate culture can drive your business success and reshape your business.

Example:

Zappos (the famous shoe e-commerce company) is a great example of a company with an exceptional creative culture.

Zappos is known for its "Happiness at Work" corporate culture. Zappos' core values are very inspiring. Here are two: "Build a positive team and family spirit" and "Pursue growth and learning".The employees also evolve in a fun working environment that strongly encourages their creativity.

- ★ Ways to build and maintain creativity:
- ★ Invest in identifying, measuring and nurturing human organizational creativity
- ★ Identify your most creative employees and inspire them
- ★ Nurture and reward the creative efforts in your company

- ★ Provide a supportive culture for creativity
- ★ Encourage your staff to be open to opportunities
- ★ Empower your team to solve customer problems

12. Competitive Market Research and Competitive Intelligence.
Competitor marketing research is the process of collecting and analyzing information about your current and potential competitors and market trends.Now it's easy to do! Even with the help of some free online competitor analysis tools, you can track everything your competitors are doing – from products to people to promotions.This allows you to find out what works for other businesses in your industry and identify market opportunities. This allows you to develop the most effective growth strategies for your business and gain competitive advantages.

Competitive market research combined with marketing intelligence gives you insights to improve several aspects of your overall business results. They also provide you with information about the industry you are in – its highlights, new players, established companies, innovations and disasters.

Examples:

Great companies know how to reap the benefits of the successes or failures of others. Google pays close attention to bugs in Yahoo's user interface.Uber capitalized on public enthusiasm for Lyft. Apple has redefined the wireless market - a category pioneered by Motorola. How do you do competitive market research?Use powerful web competitive intelligence tools

Identify areas to spy on your competitors, such as their products, employees, marketing campaigns, SEO strategies, etc. Evaluate the content on the competitor's website, such as blog posts, white papers, eBooks, videos, podcasts, press releases, case studies, etc. Investigate your competitors' social media posts

- ★ Become a customer of your competitor and buy products from the competition
- ★ Competitor customer survey
- ★ Ask your new customers who they have used before and why they have come to you

13. Choose a green strategy. Consumers around the world are becoming more and more passionate about protecting the planet. An environmentally friendly business strategy shows your customers that they do not make profits before the environment.Today, customers are willing to pay more for products and services that support the green thing.

When you become green, everything your company does should reflect its sustainability values. You cannot say that you are sustainable while doing some not sustainable activities. Example:

- ★ The Body Shop clearly states its values on its website.
- ★ I am against animal testing, defend human rights and protect the planet. And The Body Shop lives up to these values.
- ★ The message helps the company stand out from the crowd.
- ★ Some ways to go green:
- ★ Make green thinking part of your corporate culture
- ★ Do business with green suppliers
- ★ Get some relevant certificates like Leaping Bunny certification, etc. Organize a fundraiser
- ★ Make your office more environmentally friendly

14. Leverage global platforms. Are you an e-commerce business selling products online? If so, why not use Amazon's FBA service to expand your potential audience and reach global customers?

- ★ Or are you in the vacation home rental business? Then you can adopt and use platforms like Airbnb, InvitedHome, HomeAway to grow your business.Leveraging global, proven and world-renowned platforms is one of the fastest business growth strategies that you can easily adopt without much effort or investment. Find a platform that is relevant to your business and industry and use it to grow your business effortlessly.Today, online platforms have tremendous power as they connect buyers with businesses, unlock new supply and demand flows, and allow you to

★ gain valuable market insights.
★
★ How to use global platforms?
★ Decide which platform is best for your business: Amazon, Facebook, Alibaba, Uber, Upwork, Pinterest, Youtube, etc. Create marketing strategies, messages and efforts relevant to the platform
★ Analyze performance and results on any platform
★ Read and follow the best practices and guides to successfully use the platform

15. Create strategic partnerships. Do you know why small and large companies enter into long-term strategic partnerships with other companies? Not just because "two heads are better than one".There are many other reasons. For example, strategic partnerships can give you access to additional resources such as software and a large following on social media.The alliance also expands your customer base and helps you reach new markets, whether geographic or not. Example:

The collaboration between Google and Luxottica is a spectacular example of this.Tech giant Google and luxury eyewear company Luxottica have teamed up to create Google Glasses – a fantastic new solution. Their alliance has allowed Google to reach the fashion market and Luxottica the technology market.

★ How to create strategic partnerships?
★ Consider and value different types of partnerships such as strategic marketing partnerships, financial alliances, technology

partnerships, etc. Be clear about the value you want to retain and the value you can offer your partner
* Understand why your potential partners want to connect
* Work with a shared vision and principles
* Aim for proactive communication

16. Reputation Management. A reputation can be shattered or a deal can be struck. People depend on the opinions of others. Companies with a good reputation are the most trusted.

A positive reputation has enormous power. It allows a company to retain its best employees, attract and retain customers, gain more trust, minimize risk and easily enter new markets. We all know how easily a reputation can be changed these days – online – with just a few customer comments, reviews or blog posts. Every day, people rate companies with 1 to 5 reviews and comment on social media posts.Therefore, managing a good reputation is one of the indispensable strategies for business growth. Your reputation management should be solid and strong.

Example:

Sony, the Japanese conglomerate, manages its reputation immensely with strengths such as top-notch customer service; generous charitable giving focused on the arts, culture, technology, and the environment; and a pioneering range. How to maintain a good reputation?There are many ways to maintain a good reputation. For example:

* Always be honest, reliable, act with integrity, meet deadlines and accept responsibility for your actions
* Join professional groups and boards, attend industry events, speak at public events, guest lectures
* Help customers achieve their goals
* Provide first-class customer service
* Commit to the cause
* It produces high quality products

- ★ Create a blog with professional, useful, valuable and inspiring content
- • Be active on social media
- ★ Ask your customers to write reviews
- ★ Publicly respond to customer complaints
- ★ Use tools that monitor your reputation
- ★ Create a great website

17. Focus on certifications and awards. What certifications do you have that demonstrate your skills? What rewards do you have?

These questions are becoming more and more important these days. For what?Because certifications and awards confirm your business. They are a form of insurance of who you are and what you are doing. Subsequently winning awards makes your company shine and provide benefits such as boosting your reputation, attracting new customers and new employees, improving company morale, and increasing customer loyalty.

There are many types of awards your business can win. They are in categories like service, ethics, growth, employment excellence, community service, leadership, products, etc.

Examples:

Many leading companies have some of the most important and prestigious industry awards. For example, most of IBM's business growth strategies win a long list of awards and recognitions.As one of the most awarded companies in the world, IBM ensures that the brand is held in high esteem and respected by customers, employees and the general public around the world.

Any tips for winning Business Awards?

- ★ Be smart about the rewards you want to earn
- • Identify your strengths and find the appropriate rewards

- ★ Follow all instructions and rules
- ★ Provide the judges with solid evidence of your claims
- ★ Show that your product has great potential and that the business is sustainable
- ★ Be confident
- ★ never duplicate
- ★ be different

In practice, there are a large number of sustainable business growth strategies to choose from.All you have to do is select the plan that best suits your unique business!Once your organization has defined and planned its growth path, you are ready to succeed in our fast-paced environment.Sure, it's not easy to create long-term value with limited resources, but every long journey begins with a simple step, an idea and a great motivation.

While sustainable growth is one of the biggest challenges for any business, you should never stop improving your skills, both as an individual and as an organization.So sooner or later you will be rewarded. What do you think? What business growth strategies are working best tod ay?

Chapter 7. The 6 decision making framework that helps startup leaders tackle tough calls

The framework I collaborated on the selections we make, most of us like to assume we've made the "satisfactory" decision. And while the normal choices (what to have for breakfast, whether or not you read this newsletter) don't waste much intellectual energy, the choices we encounter with startups at scale are regularly much tougher: now no new round is in order questions, or as a new product feature to add to the roadmap, is heightened by a high-pressure environment without a secure internet. Where smart choices can boost your employer's prosperity and build trust in groups, terrible decisions can jeopardize company bottom lines and damage morale, sometimes irreversibly.

The dilemma of the course is that the choices at stake are rarely narrowed down so definitively. In a team, it is difficult to come to a consensus on what the "extraordinary" alternative pair method is; With too many choices, leaders can become paralyzed with indecision, wasting valuable time and opportunity. How to make an optimized choice for each pace and sophistication? Should you value data more or follow your instincts? How to reconcile the points of view of intelligent and willing actors without fanning the flames of battle?

In search of ideas, we consulted the advice of seasoned executives who have made the most difficult decisions in the development of startups and large companies. A running theme emerged: the art of decision-making isn't about constantly photographing an elusive "satisfactory" choice - it's about making the most of the facts at hand, capturing everyone's attention stakeholders and execute it with conviction. In this roundup, we've compiled six proven tools, frameworks, and principles for making quality decisions in fast-paced startups. They include strategies for distilling the information needed to make a decision, testing potential solutions, and balancing conflicting perspectives. We hope they help ease the decision-making process and shed some light on the decisions that can move your startup forward.

1. Codify a set of principles that guide the decision-making process

When a startup team is small and more or less in sync, most of the choices can be made by the founding team. But as your team grows and you reach unprecedented new milestones, you'll find that the guidelines for what makes a "good decision" begin to blur.

As COO of Stripe, Claire Hughes Johnson developed a decision-making framework that has become a shared decision-making compass for all team members, old and new. According to Johnson, you need to document concrete core principles that describe how you work.Once written, you must repeat them over and over again until they are all internalized. Stripe calls them "Operating Principles". (Many companies have "values," but Stripe wanted to separate philosophical beliefs from concrete principles that should be applied to the day-to-day running of business operations.) Two of Stripe's operating principles, as Johnson describes them, are:

THINK CONTRARY: "We care about doing things right and it often takes first principles of reasoning to get there. We work hard to detect errors in received wisdom. Rigor does not mean the not-invented-here syndrome; we are interested in the world around us and think that other companies, industries and academic fields can teach us a lot. But in many cases, progress comes by taking roads with less traffic."

TRUST AND EMPOWERMENT: "We want to work in a company with deeply good people who treat their colleagues exceptionally. People should work to empower themselves and do all they can to help each other in the short and long term.They should also be defined to take into account potential stresses. When two principles seem to conflict, the context should tell you which should take precedence. For example, "thinking hard" is critical for high-impact, irreversible decisions, but "going with urgency" is critical for low-impact decisions that can potentially be changed. That way, your basics serve more as a guide to action than a toothless list of nice things to have.It also makes it a useful rubric for hiring new hires and evaluating performance. Do the candidates have skills or experience that match your working principles? Are current employees carrying out their responsibilities in a way that will support them? You need to embed your work principles into your hiring and performance review processes to make them meaningful and memorable.

Your principles must be clear and explicitly enough for people who consult you make the same decisions as a founder of your business would do.

The principles of work play an even more important role in the training of new managers in the company. "If you're not careful, managers bring in all the rules and behaviors they had in their previous roles — and they have a huge impact on their teams," she says. "That's why we've created a different onboarding program for new leaders to make sure they really understand the different ways Stripe works based on our principles."Startup founding teams make hiring and product decisions using a set of unwritten beliefs that everyone knows and tacitly accepts, but they are never expressed or en route. It is never documented in...

"A lot of things happen organically when you're working in the same room with a small team all the time," he says. "There's a lot of informal capacity to get things done because you instantly understand what decisions are being made and how you want to deal with them. You will not be able to teach. They must be ready to figure it out.

If you're a corporate executive, do you know what those unsaid and unwritten things are? Have you categorized the common types of decisions you need to make? Have you documented the beliefs that guide you in making these decisions? If not, stop and do it now.

2. Use a matrix called "Xanax for Decision Making".As startups scale, teams grow, perspectives diversify, and problems become more complex. As Flatiron Health grew from four to 135 employees, CTO Gil Shklarski noticed a glaring staffing problem: Its CTOs were struggling to make streamlined decisions, whether negotiating with product managers or to vote in an internal debate.

In order to disrupt the decision backlog, Shklarski developed a framework based on a model he presented For the decision -making process "Among the members of his Flatiron team, he allows his team increasingly independent and fragmented to move quickly and wise through difficult decisions.

First, it is important to determine the distinction between good decisions and good decisions:Start with a basic chart, with the top two (or more) options to choose from. In the left column you will find benefits, costs and - unique - measures.

This can be a quick and structured thought process for someone making a decision on their own. But if a team collaborates through a suggestion, Shklarski suggests writing it on a whiteboard or in a Google Doc for everyone to see and collaborate on.

This book may seem like a generic pro/con list, but the real magic happens when you put it into practice. Specifically, it resides in the line labeled "Mitigations".

"The leader of the exercise should really be more of a facilitator, rather than putting their own opinions and judgments front and center," says Shklarski. "He should encourage everyone to think about and include the social considerations or ramifications of each option, not just the prepackaged causes and consequences at work. For example: Is a boss satisfied with a certain decision? Does a team get energy? Will someone who deserves exposure in the organization have a chance?

The facilitator should also ensure that no one is dominating the conversations and that everyone can document their perceived benefits and concerns. This contributes to psychological safety by promoting conversational skills.

Filling in the cost and benefit fields for each choice should be fairly easy. In particular, the cost line should also highlight the risks associated with each choice.

The only other thing to be careful about is making sure you generate enough in each column and thinking holistically about how choosing a particular path will play out in reality. Who is being helped? Who will be upset? What are the long-term effects? The short-term consequences? How will these effects change as the company grows? Really immerse yourself and project every choice into the future.

Then come to the mitigations. "Here, the facilitator should show the group how to mitigate, reduce, or distribute the risks associated with each of the options," Shklarski says. "If you haven't already, this exercise forces you and everyone else to think about what it would really be like if that option were checked.

Chapter 8.overcome communication barriers

There are a number of communication obstacles confronted in recent times by using all. The message supposed by means of the sender is not understood with the aid of the receiver in the identical phrases and feel and as a result communique breakdown occurs.It's far critical to deal and cope up with these conversation obstacles with a view to ensure clean and effective verbal exchange.As, within the previous section we have discussed the main obstacles of communique. Allow's communicate approximately how to overcome those obstacles of communique.Disposing of variations in notion: the organization have to ensure that it is recruiting proper individuals at the task. It's the duty of the interviewer to make sure that the interviewee has command over the written and spoken language.

There should be proper induction software in order that the rules of the corporation are clean to all of the employees. There should be right trainings carried out for required personnel (for eg: voice and accent schooling).

Use of simple language: use of simple and clean phrases need to be emphasized. Use of ambiguous phrases and jargons have to be averted.

Reduction and elimination of noise degrees: noise is the main conversation barrier which have to be conquer on precedence foundation. It's miles essential to pick out the supply of noise after which take away that supply.Energetic listening: listen attentively and punctiliously. There may be a distinction between "listening" and "listening to". Energetic listening manner listening to with proper expertise of the message this is heard. By using asking questions the speaker can ensure whether his/her message is known or now not by using the receiver in the identical phrases as supposed by way of the speaker.Emotional state: throughout verbal exchange one have to make effective use of frame language. He/she ought to no longer display their emotions at the same time as verbal exchange as the receiver would possibly misinterpret the message being introduced. For instance, if the conveyer of the message is in a terrible temper then the receiver might suppose that the facts being added isn't always suitable.Simple organizational shape: the organizational structure should not be complicated. The number of hierarchical tiers should be most efficient. There need to be a best span of manipulate inside the organization. Less complicated the organizational shape, more powerful may be the communique.

Avoid records overload: the managers have to recognise how to prioritize their paintings. They ought to now not overload themselves with the paintings. They should spend quality time with their subordinates and need to listen to their issues and feedbacks actively.Deliver optimistic comments: keep away from giving poor feedback. The contents of the feedback is probably terrible, however it must be introduced constructively. Constructive remarks will cause powerful communication between the advanced and subordinate.

Proper media selection: the managers have to nicely pick out the medium of communique. Simple messages should be conveyed orally, like: head to head interaction or meetings.Use of written method of conversation have to be endorsed for turning in complex messages. For substantial messages reminders can be given by using using written means of communique along with: memos, notices etc.

Flexibility in assembly the targets: for powerful conversation in an corporation the managers must make certain that the people are assembly their targets timely without skipping the formal channels of communique. There must now not be much stress on employees to fulfill their goals.

There are effective conversation which can be relevant to each written in addition to oral verbal exchange. Those are as follows:

Completeness - the communication should be entire. It should convey all statistics required by the target audience. The sender of the message ought to think about the receiver's thoughts set and bring the message for that reason. A complete conversation has following features:

Entire conversation develops and enhances recognition of an company.

Moreover, they are cost saving as no vital records is missing and no additional fee is incurred in conveying greater message if the communique is complete.

A complete communication continually gives extra statistics anywhere required. It leaves no questions inside the mind of receiver.

Whole communique allows in higher choice-making with the aid of the target market/readers/receivers of message as they get all favored and critical records.It persuades the target market.Conciseness - conciseness approach wordiness, i.E, speaking what you want to bring in least viable words without forgoing the opposite c's of communication. Conciseness is a need for powerful communication. Concise conversation has following features:

It's far each time-saving in addition to price-saving.It underlines and highlights the main message as it avoids the use of immoderate and needless phrases.Concise verbal exchange provides short and important message in constrained words to the target audience.

Concise message is extra attractive and comprehensible to the audience.

Concise message is non-repetitive in nature.

Attention - consideration implies "stepping into the footwear of others". Effective conversation need to take the audience into attention, i.E, the audience's view points, history, mind-set, training stage, and many others. Make an try and envisage your target audience, their necessities, emotions as well as problems. Make sure that the self-recognize of the audience is maintained and their feelings are not at damage. Regulate your words in message to healthy the target market's wishes whilst making your message whole. Capabilities of thoughtful communication are as follows:

Emphasize on "you" method.

Empathize with the audience and exhibit hobby inside the target market. This can stimulate a fantastic reaction from the target market.

Display optimism towards your target market. Emphasize on "what is possible" in preference to "what's not possible". Lay strain on tremendous words together with jovial, committed, thanks, heat, wholesome, help, etc.

Clarity - readability implies emphasizing on a specific message or aim at a time, in place of seeking to gain an excessive amount of right away. Readability in communication has following capabilities:

It makes information simpler.Complete clarity of thoughts and thoughts enhances the that means of message.

Clear message makes use of actual, suitable and urban words.

Concreteness - concrete communication implies being unique and clear instead of fuzzy and wellknown. Concreteness strengthens the self belief. Concrete message has following capabilities:

It's far supported with particular statistics and figures.

It makes use of phrases which might be clear and that build the reputation.

Concrete messages aren't misinterpreted.

Courtesy - courtesy in message implies the message must show the sender's expression in addition to ought to respect the receiver. The sender of the message have to be surely well mannered, judicious, reflective and enthusiastic. Courteous message has following features:Courtesy implies thinking of both viewpoints as well as emotions of the receiver of the message.Courteous message is fine and targeted at the target audience.

It makes use of phrases showing admire for the receiver of message.

It isn't always at all biased.Correctness - correctness in communique means that there are not any grammatical mistakes in communication. Accurate communication has following features:The message is precise, accurate and properly-timed.If the communique is accurate, it boosts up the confidence level.Correct message has extra impact on the target market/readers.It tests for the precision and accurateness of facts and figures used inside the message.It makes use of suitable and correct language inside the message.

Business conversation is aim oriented. The guidelines, regulations and guidelines of a business enterprise ought to be communicated to humans within and outdoor the corporation. Business communique is regulated through sure policies and norms. In early times, enterprise conversation was confined to paper-work, cellphone calls and so on. But now with creation of technology, we've cellular phones, video conferencing, emails, satellite communique to guide business conversation. Effective commercial enterprise communication helps in constructing goodwill of an organisation.

The main components of the communication method are:

CONTEXTS – at a low level, depending on the context in which the conversation is taking place. This context can be physical, social, chronological or cultural. All communication is CONTEXTUAL. Senders choose which messages to communicate in context. Sender/Coder - The sender/encoder is the person who sends the MESSAGE. Senders use symbols (expressions or graphics or visual aids) to convey a message and elicit a designated response. Example: A training manager is training a new batch of staff. The sender can be a man or a woman, a couple or a company. The sender's attitude, history, approach, skills, competencies and know-how greatly influence the message. The verbal and nonverbal cues you choose are important in determining whether or not the receiver interprets the message in the terms intended by the sender. A message is the main idea that the sender of the message wants to convey. Rather, it is the response signal of the receiver. The process of verbal exchange begins with deciding what message to convey. It is necessary to ensure that the main purpose of the message is clear. Medium is the medium used to exchange/transmit messages. The sender must choose the appropriate medium to send the message. Otherwise, the message may not be delivered to the intended recipient. It is important to choose the right communication tools to make your message powerful and to ensure that the message is effectively interpreted by the recipient. The need for a conversational environment varies according to the communication function. For example, choose a written medium if you need to convey the message to a small group, or an oral medium if you need immediate feedback from the recipient to clarify misunderstandings on the spot. Recipient/Recipient - Recipient/Recipient - The person to whom the message is intended/designated/designated. The degree to which a decoder understands a message depends on several factors, including the know-how of the receiver, the response to the message, and the encoder's dependence on the decoder. Comments - Comments are a major method of communication of interest because they allow the sender to verify the validity of the message. The sender can use the decoder to verify the correct interpretation of the message. Feedback can be verbal (through sentences) or non-verbal (in the form of smiles, sighs, etc.). It also supports notes, reports and more. This can be done in writing.

 powerful and green communique device calls for managerial skillability in delivering and receiving messages.A manager need to discover numerous boundaries to communication, analyze the motives for their incidence and take preventive steps to keep away from the ones barriers.Therefore, the primary obligation of a supervisor is to expand and hold an powerful verbal exchange system within the employer.

Even in India or America, drawing a circle with the thumb and forefinger confirms the sign "first class" or "suitable", while in Tunisia the same figure means "it can kill you", and in Japan it means. "cash"?

It should be clear to anyone looking at kinesics or frame language. Whether it's a job interview or a presentation, you need to know how to use human resources effectively.

Read on to learn about the various non-verbal components of oral communication... Eye Contact: Make constant eye contact with your target audience. However, make sure no character stares for more than 5 seconds at a time. Excessive eye movement can indicate a loss of self-confidence. Looking at people can be scary so this is not an accurate representation. Hand movements: Hand movements should not be stiff or loose, especially when shaking hands in a professional setting. An iron handshake [a very strong handshake] can indicate that a person is trying to dominate. Crossed Arms: Crossed arms indicate that one is not open to new ideas/opinions, especially when giving a presentation. However, if the interviewer crosses their arms in a personal interview, then the applicant must also cross their arms. Sitting position: Lying down on the chair is not always a good idea. Stand up straight, even if it's safe to do so. To take a place is to lose or give up interest. Gesture: Gesture is a form of non-verbal communication using body parts with or without verbal communication. Gestures include facial expressions, nods (in many cultures this is a sign of approval) and nods/shakes. Facial features: The face perfectly reflects a person's emotions. Understanding when someone is happy or unhappy, anxious, angry or excited has never been easier. In professional scenarios, it takes miles for someone to manage their appearance. For example, if a presenter feels that their presentation was not fully executed, they should no longer signal that they are giving up, but rather try to engage more participants.

Chapter 9.Breaking down limitations to boom

How best to re-ignite boom is a topic of immoderate debate in most of europe's advanced economies and in japan. Over the past decade, those nations have professional a slowdown of monetary boom at the equal time as lengthening life spans have induced their pension and health care costs to mount. A few economists have advocated lifting guidelines on competition in the many sectors wherein they remain and reforming difficult work marketplace guidelines. However such movements are resisted via those who fear they will bring about mass unemployment and smash social safety nets. Others recommend greater investment in research and development (r&d) and education to equip people with the skills to perform better fee-added obligations as extra low-cost jobs are computerized or migrate to lower-price economies.Who is right? In exploring the talk, this article makes a speciality of deliver-element obstacles to growth (call for-facet macroeconomic rules had been tested drastically some place else). After a decade of studies evaluating productivity in private location industries within the world's primary economies, our end is that the essential thing to boosting productiveness and for this reason boom is a coverage framework selling competition in all sectors.

Productiveness is paramount

Quotes of monetary increase among advanced economies have diverse during the last 15 years, growing pretty large changes in relative gdp consistent with capita (see chart 1). Because the chart shows, gdp according to capita can be damaged into gdp in line with hour labored (a tough measure of productiveness increase) and hours worked in step with capita (labor utilization). Productivity increase is in reality the number one source of gdp in line with capita increase, so policymakers have to make selling it a pinnacle priority. But, common increase has been curtailed in some of economies due to big declines in hours worked according to capita. Thus, developing jobs is critical, too.

Our studies of six major economies, the United States and Japan, suggest that broader regulatory reform in an industry increases collective productivity within these firms. The more sectors improve collective productivity, the greater the probability of higher GDP in that economy. look at europe In each of the six countries we studied, there can be a significant difference between the performance of the top performers and the world-class players in a given industry. For example, labor productivity in France and Germany is lower in most industries than in the same industry in the United States (see Chart 2). Food retail in France and mobile telecommunications in France and Germany are the most favorable exceptions.For every person the journey is distinctive, but the methods wherein we can efficaciously triumph over these barriers is commonplace to us all. The following are particular ways that you may use to triumph over these limitations and cross on to obtain your success.Focus - if you know the obstacles then you may triumph over them - 'information is power.'

Be as specific as feasible- set very precise goals and write them down to boom truth. The most acknowledged and effective technique you could comply with whilst setting dreams and this is referred to as the clever approach which stands for; unique, measurable, practicable, sensible and timed. Make sure that the desires you set meet these targets, this can increase your self assurance and motivation in attaining them. Break the intention down in to smaller steps to make it more realistic, measurable and workable and ensure you're specific in what you need to reap and set a date for its accomplishment.Believe in yourself - you ought to consider in your self and that your intention is viable, this is vital. Inform your self normal that you could do it and take particular day by day actions till you do attain it. This could then boom your self-bellief and while you do attain your purpose, you becomes more assured in your capability to attain similarly goals.

Face Your Fears, Feel Your Insecurities, Do It Anyway - Famous eBook by Susan Jeffer. By acting on your fears, you dispel the power of fear and increase your own power. This is the best way to overcome the fears that hold you back. It can be difficult at first, but the confidence and self-esteem it gives you is worth it.Allow the resulting anchors to intersect. As paradoxical as it sounds, even if you set a goal that you want to achieve, it's usually about the journey. This is where you learn about yourself and your cause and where all the memories and rewards come from. If you are too obsessed with results, you may miss out on many of these benefits and give up if you don't see immediate results. In my experience in the health and wellness industry, I've seen this all the time, so I'm sure people are aware of the short-term benefits of exercise, and there are many.

Chapter 10.The most common obstacles to business growth and how to overcome them

Almost all innovative companies encounter an obstacle in their future growth path at some undetermined point. An important part of overcoming them is to identify possible challenges in advance in order to develop an action plan. However, this is easier said than done, especially if you are a new SME or entering a brand new market.We worked with Shirley Mansfield, innovation and growth expert at Innovate UK, enabling businesses to overcome the constraints of commercial prosperity. Get expert insight on how to grow your commercial business and use the equipment you need to succeed...

What are the challenges of growing your business? Some of the most common obstacles that the businesses we help face time and time again include:

Money - loss of funds or uncertainty about financial control. Business Plans, Not Yet – Counterintuitively, companies can be too focused on their long-term dreams and forget the short-term responsibilities they need to take on to realize their next venture. Market and consumer issues - Companies often come to us after they don't have enough interest in their products and services or they can't find the right customer for their offering.Pricing and Profitability - Agencies typically come to us for help with pricing, profit margins and profitability. Adopt a business mindset – Companies often try to do all the work themselves without using contractors and outside support.Let's dive into some of these questions and the answers to them... Cash: Investments, Financing and Cash Flows

Investment constraints are a significant problem for many progressive organizations. Without the coin, business control and operation is impossible and expansion plans can be compromised. Innovate uk edge enables SMEs to understand a wide range of investment and funding opportunities, providing advice from a first-class regional, national and global resource (public and private) to help realize your innovation and growth plans.For example, many companies and SMEs are often unaware that they are eligible for R&D tax credits, where a skilled innovation and welfare professional can certainly add value. But the problem is not the constant search for investment. Organizations may also struggle with investment allocation issues. Without extensive experience in the early stages of a commercial enterprise, the information used to channel funding can be overwhelming.A consultant can help with cash flow forecasting, help control money coming in and out of the facility, and most importantly - prevent money going out!

business planning, not action

Shirley often advises her clients to "stop writing business proposals and start making plans." Sometimes commercial business owners can get so stuck in their 10-year business model that they forget the smaller steps they could be taking now to move to the next stage of their journey.

Shirley recommends creating a 90-day planning timeline to focus on the things that can be accomplished with the gift to increase the sense of accomplishment. This type of short-term training planning is often more effective because it prevents the organization from getting "stuck" with unfinished to-do lists and unrealistic future aspirations.This "plan, act, measure and improve" technique has been the secret behind many of her clients' goals. find the right market

When revenue growth slows, it's mostly a sign that you're not targeting the right market or that your sales message isn't resonating with your audience.Have you ever put yourself in the shoes of your customers? With your head down, it's easy to lose sight of consumer needs and pain points. Sometimes an outsider attitude can help you understand the changing needs of the market. In addition, Shirley's clients benefit from thinking outside the box to cut through the noise, whether they're reaching audiences directly through new media and podcasts or capturing the attention of the right people through custom letters. As your business grows and develops, you will likely need to expand into new markets to expand. Our experts can provide the real-time assistance, connections and insights you need to break into new verticals and global markets.

Sales planning, pricing and profitability

Proper pricing of raw materials for profit requires many concepts, procedures and experience. Considering profit margins, sales and advertising efforts, inventory management, and all the other factors involved in developing, growing, manufacturing, and distributing your product can be complicated.Set aside time for monetization plans and spend time riding with innovation and growth experts so you don't miss a single detail. A good sales plan will also consider the sales funnel, identify possible pain point factors and areas of the chain where customers get "stuck".

business thinking

Especially in smaller agencies, the commercial business owner's mindset and personal goals are often factors that can really drive performance. If you're moving from a company, it now covers your areas of responsibility that previously belonged to IT or customer service. This is where effective resource allocation, outsourcing and delegation become very important. Learn how to find the resources to rely on contractors and employees for day-to-day tasks so you can see your business thrive and expand.Internal and external obstacles to professional development

In addition to the challenges highlighted above, each business will face unique challenges as it grows, depending on its market, region, geographic area, and resource availability. However, there are some common themes that most organizations face at some point in their journey. These barriers can come from both internal and external sources, and understanding them is critical to overcoming them.

internal growth limit

The internal limits of total growth include;

Find the right group of employees

Access assets and materials

Failure to observe composite performance indicators of business enterprises

objection rejected

Inefficient strategy and internal infrastructure

Management issues

influencer marketing

unsustainable business model

outdated era

Lost cooperation

loss of creativity and innovation

external challenge

Harsh external conditions can create additional challenges, as today's political and financial climates are often beyond our control. However, being aware of skills challenges and being aware of the help available to UK businesses can help you thrive.

Outwardly difficult situations should include:

The impact of Brexit on supply chains

Covid-19 disorders

Prison issues including ir45 impact on contractors and virtual tax substitution

These external factors can disproportionately affect different groups. For example, over the past 12 months we have all seen the devastating impact of Covid-19 on the retail and hospitality industries, while some businesses have simultaneously seen an increase in online sales.While the boom in online sales sounds great, such a boom can wreak havoc on various areas of business. An innovative customer from the UK, Cauldron Technology, experienced this hand (although note that this was helped in 2020 when we were called the Business Europe Community). Breaking down business boundaries with Innovate UK Regions

Obstacles often arise as many small businesses that expand with enthusiasm for a concept or a new era can hit a wall while demanding some corporate control to build an industry-leading company. At the same time, it's been great to work with someone who helps other companies implement successful growth initiatives.Innovate United Kingdom Ed's expert-led services help any progressive commercial enterprise with over 500 employees and high growth potential to meet challenges and realize opportunities, including:

Solve the problem

Business enterprise approach and planning support

Connections to innovation ecosystems

benefit from an elegant property

Procurement Investments and financing

the pitching manual Looking for cooperation opportunities Find out how we can help you grow and expand.

Based on current research on e-commerce enterprises and small businesses, this paper reviews the literature and formulates a conceptual framework for the application of e-commerce enterprise methodologies. Macro factors, business sectors, corporate and managerial motivations and attitudes are investigated and then placed in a conceptual framework for the development of e-business in national and international markets. A set of research propositions are developed that go beyond the formal and prescriptive e-business frameworks provided in the Handbook of Advertising and E-Commerce. This includes the belief that companies with more entrepreneurial tendencies are more likely to engage in e-commerce than more conservative ones. Other factors include the size of the company, the age of the managers, and certain types of industry and products. It provides an actionable framework for future qualitative and quantitative facts by conceptualizing the tangible and intangible factors influencing e-enterprise development engineering.